A Robbie Reader

Meet Our New Student From
NICARAGUA

John A. Torres

Mitchell Lane

P.O. Box 196
Hockessin, Delaware 19707
Visit us on the web: www.mitchelllane.com
Comments? email us: mitchelllane@mitchelllane.com

Meet Our New Student From

Australia • China • Colombia • Great Britain
• Haiti • India • Israel • Japan • Korea • Malaysia •
Mali • Mexico • New Zealand • **Nicaragua** • Nigeria
• Quebec • South Africa • Tanzania • Zambia •
Going to School Around the World

Copyright © 2010 by Mitchell Lane Publishers

All rights reserved. No part of this book may be reproduced without written permission from the publisher. Printed and bound in the United States of America.

PUBLISHER'S NOTE: The facts on which the story in this book is based have been thoroughly researched. Documentation of such research can be found on page 44. While every possible effort has been made to ensure accuracy, the publisher will not assume liability for damages caused by inaccuracies in the data, and makes no warranty on the accuracy of the information contained herein.

To reflect current usage, we have chosen to use the secular era designations BCE ("before the common era") and CE ("of the common era") instead of the traditional designations BC ("before Christ") and AD (*anno Domini*, "in the year of the Lord").

Library of Congress Cataloging-in-Publication Data

Torres, John Albert.
 Meet our new student from Nicaragua / by John Torres.
 p. cm. — (Robbie reader. Meet our new student from)
 Includes bibliographical references and index.
 ISBN 978-1-58415-834-9 (library bound)
 1. Nicaragua—Social life and customs—Juvenile literature. [1. Nicaragua.] I. Title.
 F1523.8.T67 2009
 972.85—dc22

2009027359

Printing 1 2 3 4 5 6 7 8 9

PLB

CONTENTS

Nicaragua

The colorful Cathedral of Granada, near the shore of Lake Nicaragua, is typical of the beautiful churches located throughout the country of Nicaragua. Religion plays a major role in the everyday lives of the country's citizens.

Ms. Leavitt Makes an
Announcement

Chapter

I remember it like it was yesterday. It was a Wednesday morning at Roberto Clemente Elementary School here in Orlando, Florida. I'll bet you've heard of Orlando because of all the famous attractions like Disney's Magic Kingdom, Universal Studios, and SeaWorld.

It's a cool place to live, and I really like my school. It's named after a famous baseball player from Puerto Rico—Roberto Clemente—who died while taking supplies to a country I had never heard of. I think it's called Nicaragua (nih-kur-AH-gwah).

Anyway, that's where my story begins. You see, our fourth-grade teacher, Ms. Leavitt, made an announcement first thing that morning. She skipped taking attendance and said, "Class, take your seats. I have something exciting to tell you."

We all wondered what her announcement was going to be. We knew it would be good news, because she's really nice and she was smiling.

Chapter 1

"Okay, class, settle down," she said, before turning on her laptop computer and the linked projector. She went to the doorway and flipped off the light so that we could see the screen better.

"Oooh," said some of the kids. "Baseball."

"Not just baseball," said Ms. Leavitt. "But that man in the picture holding a baseball bat is the person after whom this school is named."

"Roberto Clemente!" I blurted out without raising my hand.

Roberto Clemente

"I knew you would get it first, Red," the teacher said, laughing. My name is Danny, but everybody calls me Red because I have red hair. "You're probably the biggest baseball fan in the entire school." Then she started impressing the class by reading a list of Roberto Clemente's baseball accomplishments. Finally, she said, "He died a hero."

"What do you mean?" asked Melanie, the smartest girl in the class.

"Well," Ms. Leavitt said, "in 1972, a tiny country in Central America called Nicaragua had a terrible **earthquake.** Many, many people died, and a lot of the capital city was destroyed."

She clicked her laptop and showed us a map of Central America, with the surrounding countries labeled. Nicaragua was between Honduras (hon-DOOR-us) and Costa Rica. There was a star on

Much of the capital city of Managua was destroyed during the 1972 earthquake.

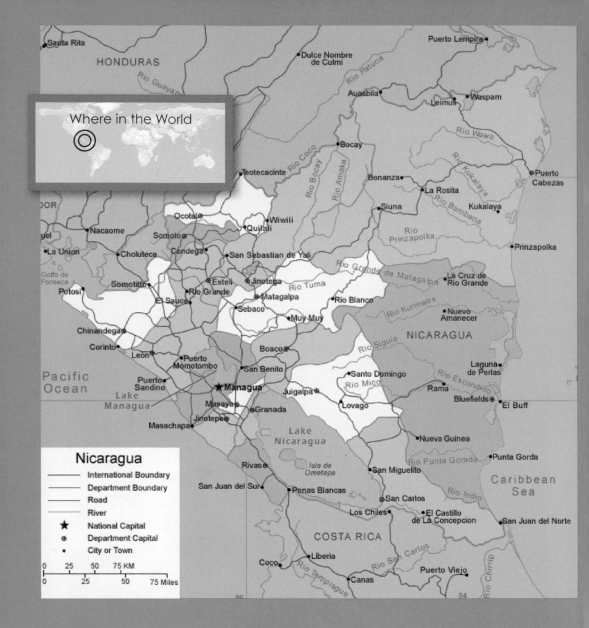

FACTS ABOUT NICARAGUA

Total Area
almost 50,000 square miles (129,500 sq km) slightly smaller than New York State

Population
5,891,200 (July 2009 est.)

Capital City
Managua

Monetary Unit
cordoba

Religions
Roman Catholicism, Evangelism, Moravianism

Ethnic Groups
mestizo (mixed Amerindian and white), white, black, Amerindian

Languages
Spanish (official), Miskito, English and indigenous languages on Atlantic coast

Chief Exports
coffee, beef, shrimp and lobster, tobacco, sugar, gold, peanuts, copper, tungsten, lead, zinc, timber, fish, textiles, apparel

Managua (muh-NAH-gwah), the capital of Nicaragua. Next she showed us photographs of Managua after the earthquake. The classroom fell silent.

After a few moments, my friend Freddy asked, "What does this have to do with a baseball player?"

"Well, some people felt the country's government was not doing enough to help during the emergency. They decided to bring relief supplies to the country by themselves."

"What are relief supplies?" I asked.

"Anything that people need to live, really, from blankets and clean water to shoes, food, and medicine," she answered. "One of the people who wanted to help was Roberto Clemente. He organized four planeloads of supplies, but the plane he was on crashed, and he died." No one in the classroom spoke as she showed photos of Clemente's family looking very sad.

"So you see," she finally said, "our little school has always had a connection to the country of Nicaragua. Now it will have another one."

The baseball world was shocked by Clemente's death.

We all looked around the room, a little bit puzzled.

"We have a new student starting today, and I want all of you to know a little bit about where he is from," she continued. "In about an hour, Ramón will walk through that door. He arrived from Nicaragua just a few days ago, and he might be a little bit shy, so I want you to be very nice to him."

León has many churches, including Iglesia El Calvario (below). The volcano Momotombo, in the background (right), erupted in 1610, destroying the first settlement in León. Now the city is the second largest in Nicaragua after Managua.

Then she spent the next sixty minutes giving us a lesson about Nicaragua. We learned all about it: what language the people speak, what kinds of food they eat, whether they celebrate any holidays, and what the kids there like to do. We would be ready for Ramón.

Nicaragua

Nicaragua's 565 miles (910 kilometers) of coast line the Pacific Ocean in the west and the Atlantic Ocean (Caribbean Sea) in the east. Nicaragua also has two large lakes: Lake Managua and Lake Nicaragua.

A Brief History of
Nicaragua

Chapter 2

Nicaragua is located in Central America, which is a strip of land that bridges North America and South America. It sits nearly halfway between Mexico and Colombia. To the north of Nicaragua is the country of Honduras, and Costa Rica lies to the south. Like the United States, Nicaragua has a coast on both the Atlantic and the Pacific oceans, but the country is only a few hundred miles across.

The land now known as Nicaragua was inhabited by Paleo-Indians more than 6,000 years ago. Preserved footprints and statues have been found that prove this. The land was named after Nicarao—a group of people who lived on the shores of Lake Nicaragua before Christopher Columbus arrived in 1502. The Spanish word for water is *agua*, so the Spanish conquerors combined both words and called the land Nicaragua. They did this because Nicaragua has so much water—from large freshwater streams to oceans on both the west and east coasts.

Before the Spaniards arrived in 1522, there were several groups of **indigenous** (in-DIH-juh-nus) peoples living in Nicaragua known as the Miskito Indians. Although the Aztecs and the Mayas lived north of Nicaragua, people who lived in western Nicaragua may have been related to these groups. Other people moved north from places like Panama and Colombia and settled on the country's east coast. They were primarily peaceful people who lived as farmers.

fun FACTS

Modern Miskito Indians still live on the Miskito Coast (along the Caribbean). Even after the Spanish conquest of Nicaragua, the Miskitos remained independent until 1894. In April 2009, as their unemployment rate rose to around 80 percent, the Miskitos declared independence again as the "Community Nation of Moskitia." They believed that if they could benefit from the natural resources of the area, such as lobsters and oil, then their economy would improve.

A Miskito Indian boy rides his horse. There are more horses than cars in much of rural Nicaragua.

When the Spanish conquerors colonized Central America, they brought weapons that were far superior to those of the indigenous people. They also brought horses—fearsome creatures that the early people had never seen before.

Everything in Nicaragua—and the western world for that matter—changed once the Spaniards arrived. Spanish settlers, explorers, and conquerors arrived on the shores of Nicaragua beginning around 1524.

Spanish culture and language spread through Nicaragua, and soon the territory became a Spanish colony. It remained a colony for a few hundred years, until the vast Spanish empire began to crumble in the 1800s. The territory declared independence from Spain in 1821, but it was not until 1838 that the

Violeta Barrios de Chamorro, part owner of the newspaper *La Prensa,* was elected president of Nicaragua in 1990. While in office, she brought an end to the Contra war and ended Sandinista control of the military.

when they elected Violeta de Chamorro as president. However, not everyone was happy with the changes. In 2006, they elected an old face when they put Daniel Ortega back in power. Technically, the country remains a **republic,** though many fear that their freedoms are being taken away, and many still live as if they are ruled by a dictatorship.

The country has enjoyed relative peace since 2006. Although it is filled with beautiful, rich traditions and hardworking people, there are still many problems in this country, including poverty, lack of health care, and fear that the government is taking freedom away.

Nicaraguan politics has often been mired in violence. In 2008, in the city of León, police clashed with supporters of President Daniel Ortega. The supporters wanted to stop a march planned by another political party.

Nicaragua

Concepción, a 5,500-foot (1,700-meter) volcano, has erupted at least 25 times since 1883. Concepción and the volcano Maderas form the island of Ometepe in Lake Nicaragua.

The Land and Its
Creatures

Chapter **3**

Nicaragua is known as the land of volcanoes. The reason is simple. There seem to be volcanoes everywhere. In fact, there are about twenty, and some are even smoking!

But this country, which is about the same size as New York State, has a lot more to offer than mountains and volcanoes. It is the largest country in Central America. There are numerous lakes, two coastlines, and even a rain forest. In fact, the country has three very distinct regions: the Pacific Lowlands, the Highlands, and the Atlantic Lowlands.

The Pacific Lowlands, in the western part of the country, are relatively flat except for a line of active volcanoes. This area is also known for the two big lakes—Lake Managua and Lake Nicaragua—that are joined by a river called Rio Tipitapa. Lake Nicaragua is the largest lake in all of Central America. Unfortunately, because of pollution, this lake is

contaminated (kun-TAA-mih-nay-ted). The government has begun cleaning up the lake to make it a tourist attraction.

Because of the rich volcanic ash, the land in certain areas is very **fertile** (FUR-tul), which means it is good for growing crops. About 30 percent of the workforce works in agriculture, growing mainly coffee, sugar, and rice.

Workers cut down sugarcane for harvesting. Sugar was introduced in the Americas by Spanish conquerors and became a major crop for Nicaragua.

Western Nicaragua is above two major undersea plates that often collide. This makes the area prone to earthquakes and volcanic **eruptions** (ee-RUP-shuns). There are usually hundreds of shocks or tiny earthquakes every year. The capital city of Managua has been destroyed twice by earthquakes. The first time was in 1931, and the second in 1972. Despite the earthquakes and volcanoes, more than half of the Nicaraguan people live in this part of the country. The main industries there are food processing, textiles, and petroleum refining.

The highlands—sometimes called the North-Central Highlands—are a mountainous area that has a much cooler climate than the Pacific Coast. This area is known for growing Nicaraguan coffee, and also for a wide variety of plants and birds. Some of the birds there include toucans, hummingbirds,

A white-faced monkey hangs out in the Nicaraguan rain forest. Made popular as "organ-grinder monkeys," these animals are often kept as pets in this country.

One of the highlights of the Atlantic coast is Nicaragua's Bosawás Biosphere Reserve. This is a government-protected plot of land that covers almost 2 million acres—or about 7 percent of the country's area. The reserve protects the largest rain forest north of the Amazon rain forest in Brazil.

The rain forest is full of wildlife. Some of the birds there include eagles, turkeys, and macaws. Animals include many types of monkeys, anteaters, and tapirs. Many of the species are protected, including the jaguar and the sea turtle.

Green turtles travel throughout the Caribbean, feeding on the sea grass beds off the coast of Nicaragua. They return to the same beaches to lay their eggs year after year.

Nicaragua

A young girl steps down from a parade float during a Purísimas festival in Granada. Purísimas celebrates the Virgin Mary, the patron saint of the country.

Religion, Customs, and
Culture

Chapter

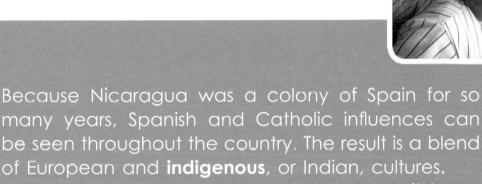

Because Nicaragua was a colony of Spain for so many years, Spanish and Catholic influences can be seen throughout the country. The result is a blend of European and **indigenous**, or Indian, cultures.

Most Nicaraguans speak Spanish, but it is not exactly the same as the Spanish spoken in other countries. That's why Nicaraguans—who call themselves Nicas—refer to their language as Nicanol. It is a sort of Nicaraguan Spanish. On the West Coast, many people still speak Miskito—the language of the Miskito Indians.

In Nicaragua, religion and tradition go hand in hand. Many of the holidays, festivals, parades, and parties are based on religion. As it is in the United States, religious freedom is guaranteed in Nicaragua. There is no official religion, but Catholics make up about 60 percent of the population. Catholic **bishops**

(BIH-shups) sometimes get involved in political matters, and they are seen as state leaders.

Following Catholic tradition, most of the small towns and cities throughout the country have a patron saint. This saint serves as a link between the people and God. Each saint has a certain day that is celebrated each year—sort of like a saint birthday party.

Festivals of the saints are huge and joyous and normally involve everyone in the town. Called *fiestas patronales*, they sometimes last for several days. They are filled with music, dancing, and food.

Three girls dress up in colorful marimba costumes for the *fiestas patronales*, or festivals for the patron saints. They will dance and possibly join a parade through their town.

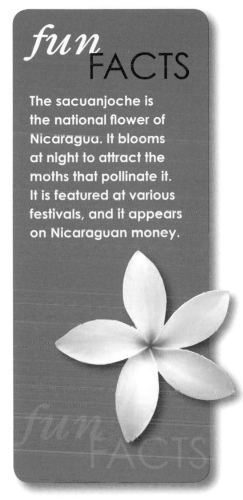

fun FACTS

The sacuanjoche is the national flower of Nicaragua. It blooms at night to attract the moths that pollinate it. It is featured at various festivals, and it appears on Nicaraguan money.

In Managua, the patron saint is Santo Domingo, or Saint Dominic. The festival for this saint lasts two days and is celebrated every August.

Food in Nicaragua is very similar to that of other Spanish-speaking countries in the Caribbean. It is a mixture of Spanish-style and Creole cooking, influenced by Africans who had been brought over as slaves after William Walker sanctioned the use of slaves in the country.

September is a festive month in Nicaragua, as the country's independence is celebrated through the entire month. The people hold parades and festivals, and hang the blue-and-white flag outside their homes. Also, a torch—burning with the fire of independence—travels throughout Central America and then into Nicaragua in time for September 15, the official day of independence.

Gallopinto

A dish of white rice and red beans called **gallopinto** (guy-oh-PEEN-toh) is served with almost every meal. Its name means "spotted rooster." It is normal to have it in the mornings with a plate of pancakes or eggs. Some people like to add coconut or other fruits to it as well. A salty cheese called *queso seco* is also a staple food in Nicaragua.

Boxing and soccer are popular sports in Nicaragua, but the most loved sport in the country is baseball. The sport was introduced in the late 1800s and early 1900s by Americans visiting the country. Several Nicaraguans have played for Major League Baseball in the United States, including David Green and Vicente Padilla. The most famous Nicaraguan player was pitcher Dennis Martinez. Known as *El Presidente* (The President), he pitched a perfect game for the Montreal Expos in 1991.

Pitcher Dennis Martinez

Nicaraguan folk music is played regularly throughout the countryside. Most of the big cities enjoy contemporary music that originates in the United States or in other Latin American countries.

One place where Nicaraguan culture has made its mark on the rest of the world is in the field of writing, or literature. The first well-known piece was a play written anonymously called *El Güegüense o Macho Ratón*. It tells the story of a merchant who outwits the government so that he does not have to pay taxes. It was seen as a slap to Spanish invaders. The play was first performed in the seventeenth century, and has become an annual tradition during the January feast of San Sabaslián, patron saint of Diriamba.

Rubén Darío, who lived from 1867 to 1916, was a world-renowned poet. He is one of the creators of modernism, a type of poetry and artwork that broke away from traditional styles in the late 1800s.

Rubén Darío is revered as Nicaragua's greatest diplomat and a leading voice of Central and South America.

Nicaragua

Ramón is excited to start school in the United States. In Nicaragua, he often had to skip school to help his father on their farm.

Ramón Arrives

Chapter 5

I had never seen our class pay so much attention to Ms. Leavitt as we did for that hour. It seemed as if everyone wanted to learn about Nicaragua. We wanted to make our new classmate feel at home.

Ms. Leavitt received a telephone call from the office and smiled. "Class," she said, "it's nearly time for lunch. Would anyone object to eating lunch right here in the classroom today?"

Everyone got excited, and Ms. Leavitt asked a few of us to help put the desks together. Before we knew it, the classroom door opened. A small boy stood there wearing a New York Mets baseball cap and holding several trays of food. I ran over to help him.

"*Gracias*," he said, with a shy smile.

"Ramón," Ms. Leavitt said as she helped with the trays as well, "what have you brought us?"

"I wanted everyone to try the most famous food of my country," he said in accented English. "It is called—"

But we all interrupted him and called out, "Gallopinto!"

He broke out into a wide smile. Before we dug into the food, Ms. Leavitt asked Ramón to tell us a little bit about his life in Nicaragua.

It turned out that Ramón was from an area called Nueva Guinea (noo-AY-vuh gee-NAY-uh). He said it was way up in the mountains. The area is very poor and hardly anyone has a car. He told us that his family had a donkey, and that was how he would get to school.

Schoolchildren in Nicaragua wear uniforms. In many schools, there are not enough materials for every student to use.

We thought it was really cool that he had a donkey. Then he told us that he also had a pig, and his father had oxen that he used to move heavy objects. We couldn't believe that he had never played a video game or surfed the Internet. But we would show him those things soon enough.

He got sad when he told us there was a lot of **poverty** (PAH-ver-tee) in his town. Not everyone there can afford to go to school. Kids need to wear uniforms, and if their parents can't afford to buy them, then they just don't go. Other families need their children to help work on their small farms.

The schools are broken down by age, just like in the U.S., but living

Roberto Clemente stadium in Masaya, Nicaragua, has been home to the Fieras del San Fernando team of the Nicaraguan Professional Baseball League. Nicaraguan baseball teams have cheerleaders and pep bands, and the noise in the stadium can be deafening. Some years, though, there is not enough money for all the teams in the league to be able to play.

As we ate our rice and beans, we talked about our favorite thing: baseball. He told me that on their way to the airport, his family passed the Roberto Clemente Stadium in Masaya. He told me about the statue of Clemente and how everyone loved him. Then it was time for recess. We ran to the baseball field together and played catch.

How To Make
Gallopinto

Gallopinto is the national dish of Nicaragua. It is even served for breakfast. Making *gallopinto* consists of three steps: cooking the beans, cooking the rice, and then combining the two. When you mix them, you'll need about twice as much rice as beans.

Because this recipe requires using a hot stove, you will need an adult to help you.

Step One: Cook the Beans

Ingredients
½ lb. dried and rinsed black beans OR
    15-oz can black beans

If using dried beans, soak the beans in a medium-sized pot for several hours, and then drain the liquid. Cover the beans with fresh water and bring it to a boil. Cook until the beans are tender, or for several hours on low heat.

Step Two: Cook the Rice

Ingredients
1½ cups long-grain white rice
2¼ cups of water or salt-free chicken
    broth
1 teaspoon of salt

Pour the rice into a medium-sized pot. Rinse the rice. Pour the water or broth over rice until the liquid is about an inch higher than the rice. Using high heat, bring the rice to a boil. Once it is boiling, cover the pot with a lid, and then lower the heat to very low. Let it simmer for 15 minutes.

Step Three: Put It Together

Ingredients
cooked rice
cooked beans
1 onion, diced
2 cloves of garlic, minced
1 red pepper, diced
1 tablespoon of oil

Using medium heat, sauté the onion, pepper, and garlic in oil. When the onions are tender, add the rice and beans. Stir until it is all very hot.

Make Your Own
Clay Piggy Bank

You Will Need

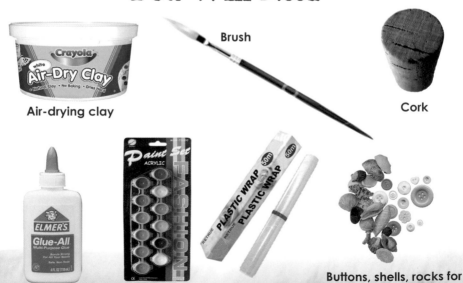

Air-drying clay

Brush

Cork

Glue

Acrylic paint

Plastic wrap

Buttons, shells, rocks for decoration (optional)

Any open-air market in Nicaragua will have dozens of choices of clay piggy banks to choose from, ranging from fancy to simple—and in many shapes besides pigs. Here is a simple way to make a clay piggy bank.

Instructions for Making a Clay Piggy Bank

1 Break off a chunk of clay and work it in your hands until the clay becomes very soft.

2 Roll the clay into a long coil.

3 Using the coil, make a base for your piggy bank. Use a little bit of water to keep the clay soft. Smooth out the coils.

4 Once your base is complete, cover it with a piece of plastic wrap.

5 Repeat the process to construct the sides of the piggy bank. Rectangular banks are easiest to make for beginners. You could also wrap coils of clay around the edges of the base, making the sides as high as you want.

6 Leave a little slit in the top for the coins. If you want, decorate it by sticking buttons, rocks, or shells in the clay, or use a table knife to draw designs in the sides.

7 Once the clay has completely dried, you can paint your bank.

Further Reading

Works Consulted
This book is based on the author's personal trip to Nicaragua in 2009. While there, he interviewed several Nicaraguans in Nueva Guinea, Masaya, and Managua. Other sources he used are listed below:

Arghiris, Richard, and Richard Leonardi. *Footprint Nicaragua (Footprint Travel Guides)*. Bath, England: Footprint Books, 2008.

Berman, Joshua, and Randall Wood. *Moon Nicaragua*. Berkeley, CA: Moon Books, 2008.

Gibbs, Stephen. "Nicaragua's Miskitos Seek Independence." BBC News, August 3, 2009. http://news.bbc.co.uk/2/hi/americas/8181209.stm

Penland, Paige, Gary Chandler, and Liza Prado. *Lonely Planet: Nicaragua and El Salvador*. Oakland and London: Lonely Planet Publishers, 2006.

Plunkett, Hazel. *Nicaragua in Focus: A Guide to the People, Politics and Culture*. Northampton, MA: Interlink Books, 2002.

Rounsefell, Erica. *Adventure Guide Nicaragua*. Walpole, MA: Hunter Travel Guides, 2007.

Central Intelligence Agency: The World Factbook: Nicaragua https://www.cia.gov/library/publications/the-world-factbook/geos/NI.html

El Güegüense o Macho Ratón http://www.vianica.com/go/specials/21-el-gueguense-macho-raton.html

"Nicaragua Baseball 2009-2010 Season Preview." Nicaragua.com. http://www.nicaragua.com/blog/nicaragua-baseball-2009-2010-season-preview

Nicaragua Channel www.nicaragua.com

Nicaragua Living www.nicaliving.com

Via Nica—Explore Nicaragua www.vianica.com

Further Reading

On the Internet
BBC News Country Profile: Nicaragua
  http://news.bbc.co.uk/2/hi/americas/country_profiles/1225218.
  stm
The Great Roberto Clemente: Latino Legends in Sports
  http://www.latinosportslegends.com/clemente.htm
El Güegüense
  http://www.diriamba.info/English/elgueguense.htm

Embassy
Embassy of Republic of Nicaragua
1627 New Hampshire Avenue NW
Washington, DC 20009
telephone: (202) 939-6570, 6573
FAX: (202) 939-6545
http://nicaragua.usembassy.gov/

Nicaraguan Cordoba

Nicaragua 5 Million
Cordobas
front (top); back (right)

Glossary

bishop (BIH-shup)—A high-ranking priest in a Catholic church.

contaminated (kun-TAA-mih-nay-ted)—Something that has been soiled or tainted.

dictatorship (dik-TAY-tur-ship)—A form of government in which all power is given to one person or a very small group.

earthquake (ERTH-kwayk)—A shaking or trembling of the ground.

eruption (ee-RUP-shun)—An explosion, such as when a volcano spews lava, smoke, and ash.

fertile (FUR-tul)—Good for growing crops.

gallopinto (guy-oh-PEEN-toh)—The most popular meal of Nicaragua, made primarily of rice and beans.

humidity (hyoo-MIH-dih-tee)—The amount of water particles in the air.

indigenous (in-DIH-juh-nus)—The first people to have lived somewhere naturally.

poverty (PAH-ver-tee)—The condition of making less money than it takes to live a normal life.

republic (ree-PUB-lik)—A government that represents the citizens who elect people to rule.

revolutionaries (reh-voh-LOO-shuh-nay-reez)—People who lead a rebellion, usually against their government.

Index

ABOUT THE AUTHOR

John Torres (center) with his son Danny Torres (right) and Dr. Francisco Ruiz of Florida at Roberto Clemente Stadium

John A. Torres is an award-winning newspaper reporter from Central Florida, and the author of more than 40 children's books, including many titles for Mitchell Lane Publishers. His stories have taken him to Zambia, Italy, Indonesia, Mexico, India, and Haiti. In 2009, he and his family traveled to the Central American country of Nicaragua. Torres found the mountains and volcanoes to be extraordinary, as were the friendliness and hospitality of the Nicaraguans. He spent a few days in Nueva Guinea and met many children like the new student Ramón in this book. He also visited Roberto Clemente Stadium in Masaya, near Managua.